My First Pet

Guinea Pigs

by Cari Meister

Bullfrog Books

Ideas for Parents and Teachers

Bullfrog Books let children practice reading informational text at the earliest reading levels. Repetition, familiar words, and photo labels support early readers.

Before Reading

- Ask the child to think about pet guinea pigs. Ask: What do you know about guinea pigs?

- Look at the picture glossary together. Read and discuss the words.

Read the Book

- "Walk" through the book and look at the photos. Let the child ask questions. Point out the photo labels.

- Read the book to the child, or have him or her read independently.

After Reading

- Prompt the child to think more. Ask: What do you need to take care of a guinea pig? Would you like to own one as a pet?

Bullfrog Books are published by Jump!
5357 Penn Avenue South
Minneapolis, MN 55419
www.jumplibrary.com

Library of Congress Cataloging-in-Publication Data

Meister, Cari, author.
  Guinea pigs / by Cari Meister.
    pages cm. — (My first pet)
  Summary: "This photo-illustrated book for early readers tells how to take care of a pet guinea pig" — Provided by publisher.
  Audience: Ages 5-8.
  Audience: K to grade 3.
  Includes bibliographical references and index.
  ISBN 978-1-62031-127-1 (hardcover) —
  ISBN 978-1-62496-194-6 (ebook) —
  ISBN 978-1-62031-145-5 (paperback)
  1. Guinea pigs as pets — Juvenile literature.
  2. Pets — Juvenile literature. I. Title.
  SF459.G9M45 2015
  636.935'92—dc23

2013045660

Series Editor: Rebecca Glaser
Series Designer: Ellen Huber
Book Designer: Anna Peterson
Photo Researcher: Casie Cook

Photo Credits: Alamy/ACE STOCK LIMITED, 10–11; Alamy/allesalltag, 16–17, 23tl; Alamy/blickwinkel, 4; Alamy/D. Hurst, 22 (water bottle); Alamy/petographer, 22 (guinea pig); Corbis/AP/Dolores Ochoa, 6–7; Getty Images/Monkey Business Images, 5; iStock, 22 (dish); Shutterstock/africa studio, 13; Shutterstock/anna karwowska, 14–15; Shutterstock/David Acosta Allely, 14 (brush); Shutterstock/Elya Vatel, 24; Shutterstock/Eric Isselee, 3; Shutterstock/Ewa Studio, 8, 23tr; Shutterstock/inkwelldodo, 9; Shutterstock/Marina Jay, 1; Shutterstock/Mark William Penny, 19 (inset); Shutterstock/Nikol Mansfeld, 20–21; Shutterstock/oksana2010, cover, 22 (shavings); Shutterstock/PhotoSky, 12, 23bl; SuperStock/CaiaImage, 18–19, 23br

Printed in the United States of America at Corporate Graphics, in North Mankato, Minnesota.
3-2014
10 9 8 7 6 5 4 3 2 1

Table of Contents

A New Pet

Jo has a guinea pig.

Her name is Honey.

Honey is lonely.
She needs a friend.
Guinea pigs do not like
to live alone.

Jo goes to a shelter.

She finds Roo.

Roo will be good for Honey.

Guinea pigs are fun.
But they need
a lot of care.

Nell and Bell are hungry.
Eve feeds them pellets.

pellets

lettuce

They eat hay and lettuce, too.

Star has long hair.
Jen brushes it every day.

Ace's cage is dirty.
Josie cleans it once
a week.

vet

Bear is sick.

Eli takes him to the vet.

He gets medicine.

medicine

Rex likes to hide.
He goes in a tube.
Peekaboo!

What Does a Guinea Pig Need?

cave
Guinea pigs like to hide under things.

water bottle
Guinea pigs need fresh water every day.

food dish
A guinea pig's food dish should be heavy so it doesn't tip over.

shavings
Guinea pigs need soft bedding and it should be changed often.

Picture Glossary

cage
A place with wire walls where a guinea pig lives and stays safe.

shelter
A place where people take care of animals that do not have homes.

pellets
Guinea pig food made of ground up plants, seeds, and vegetables.

vet
An animal doctor.

Index

To Learn More

Learning more is as easy as 1, 2, 3.

1) Go to www.factsurfer.com

2) Enter "pet guinea pig" into the search box.

3) Click the "Surf" button to see a list of websites.

With factsurfer.com, finding more information is just a click away.